NOW WE'RE COOKIN'! KIDS

Let The Kids Cook!

By Jo Anne Larzik
Illustrated by Patrick Larzik

Graphic Design by Luke Dillon
Additional Illustrations by Lacey Dillon

To my best friend Hildegarde,
who passed away in 1994, whose love of food and children we shared.

Acknowledgements

I would like to thank those who are closest to my heart. My very talented, patient husband Patrick for his wonderful illustrations and for putting up with me through all of the changes that needed to be made. My son Luke, whose incredible knowledge of graphic design and computers has brought us all into this wonderful world of technology. Lacey, "my last minute child", who came through for me when I needed her most, with those humorous illustrations. My sister Patti, who typed, read, and re-read this book (how many times?), and whose undying love and support gave me the encouragement to write this.

I love you all!

Dad, I know you are up there watching over us.

Prologue

This cookbook is written in the very precise and organized manner that I teach the children in my cooking classes (4 thru 8 year olds) at *Now We're Cookin'! Kids.*

As a parent, when I would take my young children out to dinner for a special meal, it constantly amazed me that each restaurant would offer the typical children's menu of chicken fingers, pasta with tomato sauce, grilled cheese sandwiches, or hot dogs. My preference would have been to choose among the restaurant's specialties, whether it be paella, chicken parmesan, or simply meatloaf, yet in child sized portions. I felt that children would be more apt to try different foods and perhaps acquire a taste for diversity if their typical choices were not always available.

I discovered with my own children, and subsequently while teaching children's cooking classes, that children are likely more eager to try different foods when they participate in the actual cooking of the meal. The following step-by-step, easy-to-make recipes introduce children to a variety of taste and food combinations that you and your child can prepare together.

Other cookbooks offer wonderful recipes for children, but I have yet to come across one that spells out to adults just how much children are actually capable of doing in the kitchen. My goal is to do just that. *Let The Kids Cook!*

** *Using the step-by-step instructions in each recipe, have the "Kid" follow the directions on the left side of each page and the "Grown-up" follow the directions on the right side of each page.*

TABLE OF CONTENTS

Appetizers

Soups and...

Salads and Side Dishes

Main Meals

Desserts

Drinks

STUFFED MUSHROOM CAPS
WITH DEVILED CRAB

<u>Ingredients</u>
12 large mushrooms
6 oz. shredded crab meat; fresh, frozen, or imitation
1 slice of bread
2 TBSP. softened cream cheese
½ tsp. prepared, mashed garlic
1 TBSP. chopped chives; fresh, frozen, or dried
4 TBSP. melted butter

<u>Method</u>
Pre-heat oven to 375°

<u>Kid</u>   <u>Grown-up</u>

1. Wash and dry mushrooms. Discard stems.

2. Place one slice of bread into food processor
    and pulse until only crumbs remain. Measure
    ½ C. and set aside.

3. Measure 4TBSP. butter into microwaveable
    dish. Cover and cook on high 1 minute or until
    melted.

4. Place mushrooms in one layer in shallow baking dish. Drizzle melted butter over them.

5. Cover with plastic wrap and cook in microwave, on high, 2 minutes.

6. Remove plastic wrap immediately and let cool.

7. Slice chives, thinly.

8. Measure 2 TBSP. cream cheese and place in medium mixing bowl.

9. Add to cream cheese: 1 TBSP. chives, $\frac{1}{2}$ tsp. mashed garlic, 6 oz. crab meat, and $\frac{1}{2}$ C. bread crumbs. Mix thoroughly until thick and sticky.

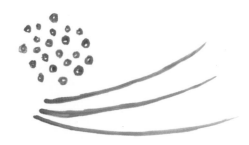

10. Using a spoon, fill mushroom caps with crab mixture. Using your fingers, lightly press filling into caps to secure. Place mushrooms back into baking dish.

11. Place mushrooms in oven. Bake 15 minutes or until topping is starting to brown. Remove.

HAM AND CHEESE SPIRALS

Ingredients
1 sheet puffed pastry, thawed
$\frac{1}{4}$ lb. thinly sliced ham
4 TBSP. dijon mustard, sweet-hot mustard,
      or barbeque sauce
4 TBSP. grated parmesan cheese
1 egg
1 TBSP. water

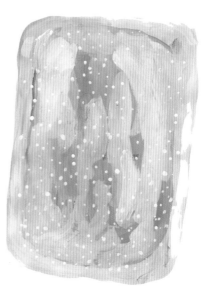

Method
Preheat oven to 400°

Kid

3. Wet a piece of paper towel. Squeeze out all of the water and cover one half of the pastry with dampened towel to use later.

4. Measure $\frac{1}{4}$ C. mustard (or barbeque sauce) and $\frac{1}{4}$ C. parmesan cheese.

5. Using a basting brush, spread 2 TBSP. of mustard (or sauce) onto the unrolled pastry to within 1 inch of the edges.

6. Lay half of the ham slices, slightly overlapping the pieces, on top of the sauce.

7. Sprinkle 2 TBSP. of cheese on top of ham.

8. Roll up the pastry from the long side (jelly roll fashion). Repeat with remaining pastry and ingredients.

Grown-up

1. Unroll thawed pastry sheet onto lightly floured surface.

2. Cut in half, horizontally.

3

9. Cut pastry logs into ½ inch pieces (approx. 15 slices each).

10. Lay spirals flat, 1 inch apart, on baking sheet lined with parchment paper.*

11. Crack egg and mix well with 1 TBSP. water using wire whisk.

12. Using a clean basting brush, lightly spread egg wash onto ham spirals.

13. Bake spirals approx. 15 minutes or until golden brown and puffed.

14. Cool 5 minutes before removing from baking sheet.

*Spirals can be frozen at this point and baked at a later date.

CORN CHOWDER WITH DICED TOMATOES

Ingredients

2 large ears of fresh corn
1 TBSP. butter
½ C. finely chopped shallots (2 lg.)
2 cloves minced garlic
1 celery stalk
1 carrot peeled
1 14½ oz. can chicken broth
¼ tsp. black pepper
½ tsp. salt
1 TBSP. dried sage
1½ C. half & half or 1 C. heavy cream
1 28 oz. can diced tomatoes, well drained
1 TBSP. flour and 2 TBSP. water if needed*

Method

Kid

1. Remove husks from corn cobs. Wash corn cobs.

3. Peel and wash carrot. Wash celery stalk.

4. Peel** garlic clove and shallots. In food chopper, chop garlic clove. Remove. Chop enough shallots to measure ½ C..

5. Measure salt, pepper, and sage, and combine in one bowl.

Grown-up

2. Cut kernels off corn cobs. Place in bowl and set aside. Do not discard cobs.

6. Cut carrot and celery into 2 inch pieces.

7. Open can of chicken broth and can of tomatoes.

5

8. Pour diced tomatoes into strainer over sink and let drain until ready to use.

9. Measure 1 TBSP. butter and put into the pot.

10. Melt butter in pot over medium/high heat. Add mashed shallots and garlic to butter. Cook until tender (5 minutes). Remove pot from heat.

11. With adult supervision: Wearing oven mitts and apron, add carrots, celery, spices, and chicken broth to pot.

12. Break corn cobs in half. Add to pot. Stir.

13. Raise heat and bring mixture to a boil for one minute. Lower heat and cook 10 minutes more.

14. Remove and discard carrots, celery, corn cobs.

15. Add corn kernels and cook for 15 minutes on low heat.

16. Add drained tomatoes.

17. Measure 1½ C. half & half (or 1 C. heavy cream). Pour slowly into soup pot. Stir while heating thoroughly, but do not boil.

*If not thick enough, dissolve 1 TBSP. flour into 2 TBSP. water. Mix into soup. Stir constantly until thickened.

**Place garlic clove on flat surface. Using heavy small pot or skillet, smash clove for easy removal of outer skin.

Carrot Soup

Ingredients

3 C. peeled carrots, cut into 1" pieces
    (approximately one 1 lb. bag)
$\frac{1}{4}$ C. finely chopped onion
2 $14\frac{1}{2}$ oz. cans of chicken broth
1 tsp. dried tarragon
1 bay leaf
2 TBSP. butter, separated
1 TBSP.
$1\frac{1}{2}$ C. half & half

Method

Kid

1. Peel and wash carrots.

3. Chop onion in food chopper
   to measure $\frac{1}{4}$ C..

5. Measure 1 TBSP. butter and put into a
   4 quart pot.

6. Measure 1 tsp. tarragon.

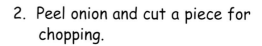

Grown-up

2. Peel onion and cut a piece for
   chopping.

4. Cut carrots into 1 inch pieces.

7. Open cans of chicken broth.

8. Melt butter in pot with onion and
   cook until tender (approx. 5
   minutes).

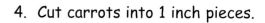

7

9. Wearing an apron and oven mitts, add tarragon, bay leaf, chicken broth, and carrots into butter/onion mixture. Stir and cover pot.

10. Lower flame and simmer 20 minutes or until carrots are tender. Do not undercook carrots.

11. Set up food processor.

12. Remove bay leaf.

13. Pour soup into food processor (may need to be blended in two batches).

14. Using the pulse button, blend the soup until pureed (no whole ingredients remaining).

15. Measure 1 TBSP. flour.

16. Melt remaining 1 TBSP. butter in pot over medium/high heat. Stir in flour until thick and smooth.

Together:
17. Pour pureed soup into pot and combine with butter/flour paste until thickened.

18. Add half & half slowly into soup, stirring until heated through, but not boiling.

Serve with pita crisps.

PITA CRISPS

Ingredients
1 round pita bread
1 TBSP. butter
1 TBSP. olive oil
2 TBSP. grated parmesan cheese

Method
Pre-heat oven to 375°

Kid

1. Measure 1 TBSP. butter and 1 TBSP. olive oil into microwaveable bowl. Cover and heat until melted, approx. 1 minute on high.

3. Brush each pita half lightly with oil mixture. Sprinkle with grated cheese.

6. Line baking sheet with parchment paper. Place wedges on baking sheet.

Grown-up

2. Using a knife, split the pita bread in half (horizontally).

4. Using a knife or pizza cutter, cut each pita half into 8 wedges.

5. Cut parchment paper to fit baking sheet.

7. Place baking sheet in oven. Bake for 8 - 10 minutes or until edges are just browned. Remove.

VOLCANIC SALAD WITH DIJON SHALLOT VINAIGRETTE

Ingredients

1 large baking potato
4 slices of bacon
2 TBSP. butter
salt, pepper, & paprika to taste
6-8 C. mixed green leaf lettuces
1 yellow pepper
½ cucumber
12 grape or cherry tomatoes
1 lg. pear
6 oz. crumbled blue cheese
1 C. Honey Roasted Pecans*
Dijon Shallot Vinaigrette**

Method

This salad recipe takes a bit more time than most green salads, but it's worth every minute. Make sure that you and your child have the time to spare before getting started, or prepare recipe in stages ahead of time.

Preheat oven to 400°

Kid	Grown-up

1. Peel 1 lg. potato.

2. Place 4 bacon slices on microwavable dish and cover with paper towel. Cook on High about 4-5 minutes or until bacon is crisp. Let cool. Crumble bacon and set aside.

3. Cut and dice potato into ½ inch cubes. Place in a small mixing bowl.

4. Measure 2 TBSP. butter and melt, covered, in microwave on High for one minute.

5. Pour melted butter over potato cubes. Mix until well coated.

10

6. Arrange potatoes in single layer in a shallow baking dish. Sprinkle with salt, pepper, and paprika.

7. Place potatoes in oven. Bake 45 minutes. Remove. Reduce oven to 325 degrees.

8. Using a salad spinner, wash 6-8 C. of salad greens and spin until dry. Place greens in large salad bowl.

9. Wash and dry yellow pepper & tomatoes. Wash and peel cucumber.

10. Slice pepper and ½ of cucumber.

11. Add vegetables to salad. Add crumbled blue cheese to salad. Toss well.

12. Cover salad and place in refrigerator.

13. Wash pear. Do not peel.

14. Quarter & core the pear. Cut each quarter into 4-5 slices. Chill until ready to use.

*Honey Roasted Pecans:

15. Measure ½ C. pecan halves and place in small bowl.

16. Coat with 1 TBSP. oil (vegetable or olive). Using oiled spoon, measure 2 TBSP. honey and pour over nuts. Toss until well coated.

17. Sprinkle 1 tsp. sugar over nut mixture. Toss.

18. Place nuts in single layer on parchment paper lined cookie sheet.

19. Bake nuts in 325 degree oven for 12-15 minutes, or until lightly browned. Cool completely.

(Nuts can be stored in airtight container for up to one week.)

Dijon Shallot Vinaigrette Dressing:

20. Peel shallot. Place in vegetable chopper and process until shallot is finely chopped or mashed. Put in small bowl.

21. Measure the following into the bowl with shallots:
    3 TBSP. tarragon flavored white wine vinegar
    ½ tsp. dijon mustard
    1 tsp. prepared mashed garlic
    ½ tsp. salt
    1/3 C. olive oil

22. Whisk all ingredients together well.

Assembling the salad:

23. Divide the warm potatoes among four salad plates, placing them in the center.

24. Toss the salad greens with dressing (keeping 3-4 TBSP. of dressing set aside). Arrange in mounds over potatoes.

25. Sprinkle bacon and honey roasted pecans on top. Arrange pear slices around salad mounds. Drizzle remaining dressing on top of nuts and pears.

Serve immediately.

PASTA PESTO SALAD

Ingredients

10 oz. cooked & cooled penne pasta
1 C. diced ham
1 C. diced, fresh tomatoes
½ C. mayonnaise
2 TBSP. prepared pesto sauce
1 tsp. prepared mashed garlic
1 tsp. dijon mustard
2 TBSP. parmesan cheese
salt & pepper to taste
2-3 TBSP. toasted pinenuts

Method

Kid

1. Fill 4 quart pot halfway with water.

Grown-up

2. Place pot on stovetop and heat until water is boiling.

3. Add 10 oz. penne pasta plus 2 TBSP. vegetable oil (to prevent pasta from sticking together).

4. Cook until pasta is "al dente", approximately 12 minutes.

5. Drain cooked pasta into colander. Rinse immediately in cold water to prevent over-cooking.

6. Measure mayonnaise, pesto, garlic, mustard, and cheese into a large bowl. Mix all ingredients together with a spoon until creamy.

7. Add cooled penne pasta and combine well. Add salt & pepper to taste.

8. Dice ham and tomatoes.

9. Add ham and tomatoes to bowl and mix gently. Chill in refrigerator at least 2 hours.

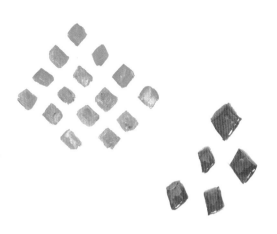

10. Measure 2-3 TBSP. raw pine nuts into small baking tin.

11. Bake nuts in 375 degree oven for 2-3 minutes until golden. <u>Watch carefully</u>! Remove and cool nuts.

12. Just before serving, toss pasta salad with toasted pinenuts.

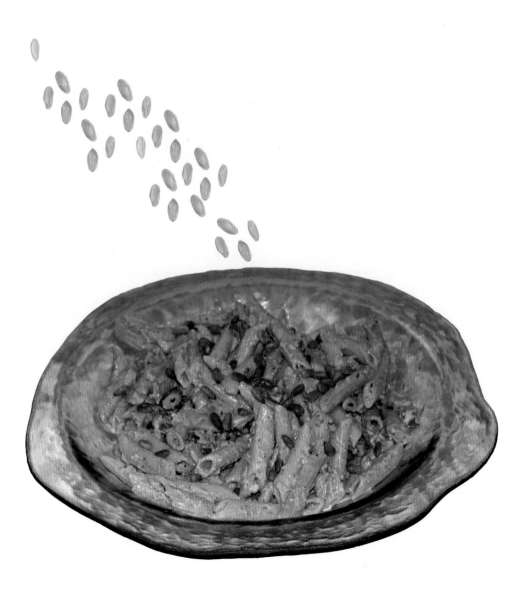

MASHED POTATOES

Ingredients

2 lbs. medium baking potatoes (about 4)
1/3 C. heavy cream
1/3 C. grated parmesan cheese (preferably asiagio)
1 stick butter, room temperature
1 tsp. salt
More salt & pepper to taste

Method

Preheat oven to 375°

Kid

1. Wet the potatoes and peel*.

3. Put cut potatoes in 3-4 quart pot. Cover with cold water.

5. Measure 1/3 C. heavy cream and 1/3 C. grated parmesan cheese, separately.

Grown-up

2. Cut potatoes into 1 inch pieces.

4. Place pot on stovetop, cover, & heat until boiling. Reduce heat and cook 20 minutes or until fork can insert easily into potatoes. Drain potatoes in colander and transfer to a large mixing bowl.

6. Add butter, cream, parmesan cheese and salt, all at once, to potatoes.

7. Using an <u>electric mixer</u>, whip potatoes on high speed until all ingredients are well blended and potatoes are creamy.

8. Add more salt & pepper to taste.

9. Transfer potatoes to oven proof baking dish.

10. Bake in 375 degree oven for 25 minutes. Top will be lightly browned.

*Wet the potatoes first, it makes them easier to peel.
To save time, both adult and child may want to peel the potatoes together.

PAELLA

Ingredients

½ lb. medium uncooked shrimp, fresh or frozen/thawed
2 chicken breast halves, skinned and boneless
4 TBSP. olive oil
3 links of sweet sausage
1 medium onion
2 cloves garlic
2 C. chicken broth
1 C. uncooked spanish rice (or long grain white rice)
1 tsp. dried oregano
½ tsp. paprika
½ tsp. salt
¼ tsp. pepper
1/8 tsp. ground turmeric
1 medium sweet red pepper
¾ C. frozen peas
1 14½ oz. can diced tomatoes, not drained

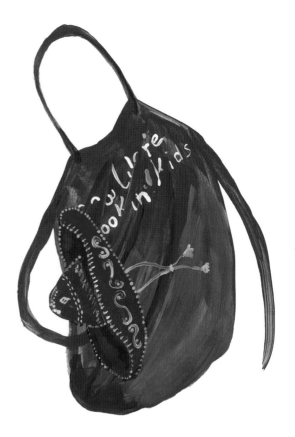

Method

Kid

1. Remove shells (and tails if desired) from shrimp.

3. Wash and pat dry shrimp and chicken breasts.

4. Place sausage on microwave-proof dish. Cover with paper towel. Cook 4 minutes on high power.

Grown-up

2. De-vein shrimp by making a shallow slice along curved back. Remove any debris.

5. Slice sausage into ½ inch pieces and set aside.

6. Cut chicken breasts into 1 inch cubed pieces.

17

7. Heat 2 TBSP. oil in 4 quart pot. Cook chicken until just browned on all sides. Remove and set aside. Cook shrimp in same pot until just light pink. Remove and set aside.

8. Remove outer layer paper from onion and garlic*.

9. Cut onion into pieces small enough for food chopper.

10. Chop onion** and garlic together until pieces are coarse.

11. Measure 2 C. chicken broth.

12. Measure all spices into small bowl.

13. Add remaining 2 TBSP. oil to pot. Cook onion and garlic until softened(about 5 min).

14. Using oven mitts and apron, add chicken broth, rice and spices to pot, stir to combine.

15. Heat mixture until boiling, reduce temperature to simmer. Cover. Cook 20 min.. Stir occasionally.

16. Cut red pepper in half, lengthwise.

17. Clean out inside of red pepper, removing all seeds. Wash.

18. Slice pepper into strips.

19. Measure ¾ C. peas.

20. Add all remaining ingredients, except shrimp, to pot. Stir well. Cook, covered, 5 - 7 minutes. Add shrimp, stir, and heat until shrimp is completely cooked (5-7 minutes).

* Place garlic clove on flat surface. Using heavy small pot or skillet, smash clove for easy removal of outer skin.
** Holding a small piece of bread between your lips while chopping onions helps absorb the stinging vapors to prevent eyes from tearing.

MOUTHWATERING MEATLOAF

Ingredients

1 egg
½ C. bread crumbs
1 tsp. dried basil
½ tsp. oregano
¼ tsp. garlic powder
1/3 C. tomato sauce
    + 1/3 C. tomato sauce for topping
1½ lb. lean ground beef

Method

Preheat oven to 400°

Kid

1. In a medium sized bowl, mix first 5 ingredients with a fork.

2. Mix in 1/3 C. tomato sauce.

3. Mix in ground beef, using your hands, to combine thoroughly.

4. Shape into large ball and place into a greased 9 inch baking dish or loaf pan. Flatten slightly and shape into a loaf.

6. Spoon remaining 1/3 C. sauce on top of meatloaf.

Grown-up

5. Place pan in oven and bake for 50 minutes. Remove from oven.

7. Bake for an additional 10 minutes.

CHICKEN PARMESAN

Ingredients

6 chicken breast halves, skinless & boneless
½ C. flour
1 egg beaten with 1 TBSP. water
¾ C. seasoned bread crumbs
1½ C. tomato sauce
½ tsp. each: garlic powder, basil, oregano
1½ C. shredded mozzarella cheese
salt & pepper to taste
4 TBSP. vegetable oil

Method

Kid

1. Rinse chicken under cold water. Pat dry with paper towels.

2. Lay chicken pieces flat on a plate and season with salt & pepper.

3. Have 3 shallow bowls ready:
   bowl 1 - measure ½ C. flour
   bowl 2 - mix egg with 1 TBSP. water
            using a wire whisk
   bowl 3 - measure ¾ C. bread
            crumbs

4. In the following order, coat both sides of chicken:
   a. dredge chicken in flour to coat
   b. dip into egg mixture to coat
   c. lay in bread crumbs to coat

Grown-up

5. Heat 4 TBSP. oil in large frying pan.

6. Place each coated piece of chicken in pan. Cook over medium/high heat about 2-3 minutes until golden brown. Turn each piece over once and cook for 2 minutes.

21

7. Remove from burner.

8. Mix tomato sauce and spices together. Pour over browned chicken breasts, making sure that sauce seeps under the chicken too.

9. Return pan to stovetop. Cover and cook for 25 minutes on medium/low heat.

10.　　Measure mozzarella cheese.

11. Uncover pan after 25 minutes and sprinkle cheese on top. Cover and cook until cheese melts (approx. 5 mins.).

CREAMY POT LUCK VEGETABLE CASSEROLE

Ingredients

6 oz. of your favorite pasta: rotini, penne, ziti
3 C. (total) cooked vegetables: broccoli, corn,
     zucchini, artichoke hearts, etc...
2-3 tomatoes, remove as many seeds as possible
1 small onion
1 clove minced garlic
4 TBSP. butter, divided
2 TBSP. flour
$\frac{1}{2}$ C. chicken broth
$\frac{1}{2}$ C. milk
$\frac{1}{2}$ tsp. salt
1 tsp. dried basil *or* 2 tsp. freshly chopped
1 tsp. oregano *or* 2 tsp. freshly chopped
$\frac{1}{4}$ C. fresh parsley
$\frac{1}{2}$ C. shredded cheddar cheese
$\frac{3}{4}$ C. fresh bread crumbs
$\frac{1}{2}$ C. shredded muenster cheese

Method
Preheat oven to 375°

Kid   **Grown-up**

1. Measure 6 oz. of pasta.

2. Cook pasta (al dente). Drain and transfer to casserole dish.

23

3. Measure 3 C. cooked vegetables. Set aside.

4. Cut up tomatoes and set aside.

5. Slice onion.

6. Measure all spices together into a small bowl. Set aside.

7. Measure ½ C. chicken broth.

8. Place 2 TBSP. butter in same pot used for cooking pasta.

9. Place pot on stove top and heat on medium/high until butter is melted.

10. Add onion and cook for 5 minutes. Add garlic and cook for 1 minute more.

11. Wearing an apron and oven mitts, add 2 TBSP. flour to melted butter. Stir with wooden spoon until smooth.

12. Add all spices, salt and chicken broth. Stir until thickened.

13. Measure ½ C. milk and add to sauce. Stir until smooth (approx. 2 min.).

14. Remove pot from stove-top.

15. Add cooked pasta, vegetables, and parsley. Mix well into sauce.

16. Measure cheeses and sprinkle on top. Add tomato pieces. Gently combine into pasta mixture.

17. Pour mixture into 9" x 13" casserole dish. Bake uncovered for 20 minutes.

18. Measure remaining 2 TBSP. butter into a microwaveable bowl. Cook on high for 1 minute or until melted.

19. Measure ¾ C. bread crumbs into bowl with melted butter and stir until combined.

20. Remove casserole from oven after 20 minutes.

21. Sprinkle buttery crumbs on top of casserole.

22. Return casserole to oven and bake 8 - 10 minutes longer.

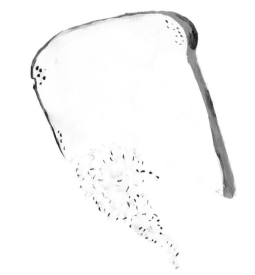

ICED BANANA CAKE

Ingredients

3 C. flour
1¼ C. sugar
4 medium over-ripe bananas, peeled and broken into pieces
¾ C. butter or margarine, room temperature
1tsp. plus ½tsp. each: baking powder & baking soda
2 tsp. vanilla
2 egg
* Icing

Method
Preheat oven to 350°

Kid

1. Measure 3 C. flour, 1¼ C. sugar, ¾ C. butter (or margarine) 1tsp. plus ½tsp. each; baking soda and baking powder, into the mixing bowl of an electric mixer.

2. Into a separate small bowl, crack 2 eggs. Add 2 tsp. vanilla. Whisk together, slightly.

3. Peel all 4 bananas, making sure to remove any of the strings that stick to the fruit from its skin. Add to large mixing bowl.

4. Add egg mixture to mixing bowl. Beat on low speed until just combined. Beat on medium/high for 1 minute. Scrape mixture from sides and bottom of bowl with a rubber spatula and beat for 2 more minutes.

5. Grease a 10" x 15" x 2" sheet cake pan using either butter, or oil spray.

Grown-up

26

6. Pour all banana batter into the prepared pan and spread evenly with a rubber spatula.

7. Place pan in oven and bake for 22-25 minutes or until an inserted toothpick comes out clean. Cool completely.

8. Spread *icing over cake.

9. Cut cake into squares.

*BANANA CAKE ICING

Ingredients

1 16 oz. box confectioner's sugar
½ C. butter or margarine at room temperature
2-3 TBSP. milk, if needed

Method

Kid

1. In a large mixing bowl, pour in 1 box of confectioner's sugar.

2. Measure ½ C. butter or margarine.

3. Add to mixing bowl.

4. Using an electric hand mixer, beat mixture on low speed until just combined. Beat again on High until smooth and creamy. If needed, add milk, 1 TBSP. at a time to achieve desired spreading consistency.

Grown-up

APPLE CRISP

Ingredients

3 Golden Delicious apples

3 Granny Smith apples
   (or mix and match your choice of baking
   apples: Jonagold, Crispin, Macintosh, etc.)

$\frac{3}{4}$ C. dark brown sugar

$\frac{3}{4}$ C. flour

$\frac{1}{2}$ C. butter at room temperature

$\frac{1}{2}$ tsp. cinnamon

1 C. quick cook oatmeal

Method
Preheat oven to 350°

Kid   ## Grown-up

1. Peel all 6 apples*.

2. Measure $\frac{3}{4}$ C. packed** brown sugar. Put into
   medium mixing bowl.

3. Measure $\frac{3}{4}$ C. flour. Add to sugar.

4. Using a fork, combine the flour with the
   brown sugar, breaking apart any sugar lumps.

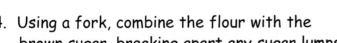

5. Measure $\frac{1}{2}$ tsp. cinnamon and add to flour
   mixture. Combine well.

6. Measure $\frac{1}{2}$ C. butter or margarine.

7. Using a fork or pastry cutter, combine
   butter with flour/sugar mixture until
   everything sticks together.

8. Measure 1 C. oatmeal. Add to flour/sugar/ butter mixture. Using finger tips, squish everything together until sticky crumbs are formed.

9. Cut apples in half and core. Cut into $\frac{1}{4}$"- $\frac{1}{2}$" slices.

10. Butter a 9" x 13" baking dish.

11. Layer dish with apple slices.

12. Spoon crumb mixture over apples.

13. Place dish into oven and bake for 40-45 minutes or until top crumbs are browned.

Serve warm with vanilla ice cream!

*Apples are one of the more tedious fruits to peel. To save time, adult and child may choose to peel apples together.

**Packed Brown Sugar means pressing sugar down into the cup until you reach the desired measurement.

OLD FASHIONED LEMONADE

Ingredients for lemon syrup*

8 C. water
1 C. sugar
8 lemons

Method

Kid

Grown-up

1. Measure 8 C. water and 1 C. sugar. Place in pot.

2. Heat and stir sugar/water on stovetop until sugar dissolves.

3. Cut lemons into halves.

4. Using a juicer, squeeze juice out of all lemons. Keep 3 of the half lemon rinds.

5. Using a small sieve to remove all seeds, pour lemon juice into pot of warmed sugar/water.

6. Add the 3 half lemon rinds. Stir.

7. Let mixture cool completely.

8. Remove lemon rinds.

To serve: Add equal parts of lemon syrup and ice water into pitcher.

*Lemon syrup can be saved in refrigerator for up to one week.

We are the future chefs of the world!
Let us cook!

Spoon Stickers

Place the correct color-coded stickers on your own measuring spoons. Your spoons will then coordinate with colored measurements in the following recipes.

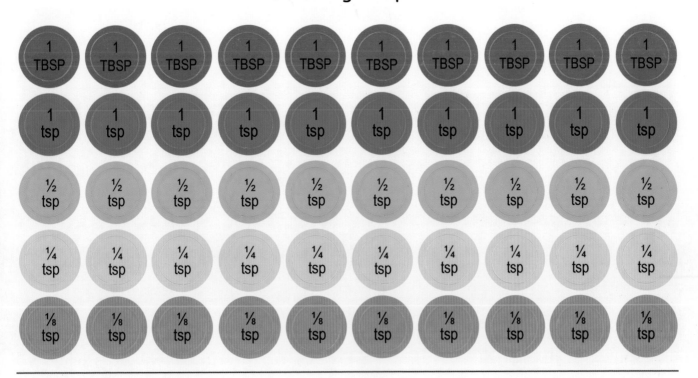

1 TBSP	1 TBSP	1 TBSP	1 TBSP	1 TBSP	1 TBSP	1 TBSP	1 TBSP	1 TBSP	1 TBSP
1 tsp	1 tsp	1 tsp	1 tsp	1 tsp	1 tsp	1 tsp	1 tsp	1 tsp	1 tsp
½ tsp	½ tsp	½ tsp	½ tsp	½ tsp	½ tsp	½ tsp	½ tsp	½ tsp	½ tsp
¼ tsp	¼ tsp	¼ tsp	¼ tsp	¼ tsp	¼ tsp	¼ tsp	¼ tsp	¼ tsp	¼ tsp
⅛ tsp	⅛ tsp	⅛ tsp	⅛ tsp	⅛ tsp	⅛ tsp	⅛ tsp	⅛ tsp	⅛ tsp	⅛ tsp

I can cook!

#1 CHEF

8oz.
6oz.
4oz.
2oz.

I can measure!

MiLk

I eat healthy!

#1 CHEF

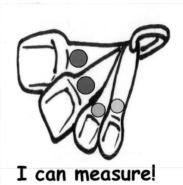

I can measure!